TABLE OF CONTENTS

CHAPTER 1

Introduction

Introduction
A primer to help you create a world-class brand identity

Based on both extensive research and practical application within organizations of all sizes, both in the US and in Europe over the last 15 years, this book is specifically designed for forward-thinking, inspired and brave business leaders who lead, or seek to lead, forward-thinking, inspired and brave organizations.

Of course, almost all of us would say that we are indeed leaders who comprise all of these qualities and that our organization is already functioning along normal, accepted parameters. But I am going to challenge your notion of what it means to be forward-thinking, inspired and brave. While many leaders and organizations may already have a compelling product or service and have built fantastic business models to supply that product or service to a market that is clearly demanding such, we are always looking to improve.

The nexus of this challenge concerns the strength of your company's brand, or brand identity. The simple fact of the matter is that you might have the best product or service on the market today, but unless your brand identity is compelling on multiple levels, and creates deep and meaningful engagement with your Customers, Employees, and Stakeholders, it is not performing to its true potential. In an intensely competitive environment, this underperformance could prove costly.

The reality is that the brand identities of the vast majority of companies on the market today are not meeting most of the *real* needs of their Customers, Employees, and Stakeholders. What are these *real* needs? We will get to these later on. But these real needs represent a demand. Since *most* organizations are lacking in supplying this demand, there is a fantastic opportunity for your company's brand identity to meet these needs and set yourself apart in a field of unending sameness.

With this book, I am first going to present you Simple Truths, and how these lead to your Opportunity, and Your Rewards. I will then present the Ground Rules for Success, and finally a How-to Guide for creating the essence of what will prove to be a very hard-to-copy, world-class brand identity from which you can grow, and lead, your industry.

To be clear, this book *will not* appeal to everybody. This is because it digs very deeply into notions that are typically off-limits in the traditional organizational mindset. This book *will*, however, appeal to the people who do want to dig deeper into what creates real engagement and fulfillment, and how to associate these two powerful assets with your company's brand identity. It will require an open mind, courage and resolve. But once you start this journey, and stay the course with uncompromising authenticity and enthusiasm, you will create the foundational essence for your company's brand identity that will outperform the general market, your industry peers, and open vast new oceans of value creation potential for your company. This, in turn, will have incredibly positive impacts on your company's productivity, efficiency and overall profitability. It all starts with your company's brand identity.

Let's begin.

CHAPTER 2

Simple Truths
(and the Elemental Forces at Play)

Simple Truths
(and the Elemental Forces at Play)

In today's hypercompetitive business environment, your company's brand identity is more important than ever. To create a powerful brand identity, you need to keep in mind some simple truths. The truths that I am about to present are obvious to many of us but are forgotten in the pursuit of keeping things simple. I understand this tendency simply because, in our day-to-day, we have very little time to delve into the more nuanced.

But to create a world-class brand identity, and one that stands head and shoulders above the rest in an environment of unending sameness, your organization will need to embrace the below points. I call them "Simple Truths". They are essential to keep in mind at all times during your brand's evolution in order to create powerful magnets that attract, sustain and delight the most engaged attention of your three main target segments (which I will get into later).

Here are the Simple Truths:

- **Learning, Growth, Expansion, and Evolution**
  As human beings, it is our nature to grow and evolve. In fact, the very nature of the cosmos itself is growth, expansion, increasingly complex systems, and evolution. Yes, destruction is also a part of the cosmos, but this makes room for the increasingly complex systems and evolution that I just mentioned. These forces are elemental in the cosmos and are represented in what we experience at the local level right here on planet earth, and in every single human civilization that has ever existed.

- **Love**
  In the spectrum of human emotion, there are two polar opposites: Love and Hate. Love is associated with light, belonging, happiness, health, creativity, growth, vibrancy and life itself.

  Hate is associated with darkness, separation, sadness, ill-health, suffering, and destruction.

  Love feels airy, while hate feels heavy. Love attracts the loyalty of others. Hate, while it may appear to attract the loyalty of others who also feel hate, is based on weak foundations that will undoubtedly crumble over time.

- **Happiness and Fulfillment**
  The vast majority of human beings are on a continuous quest for Happiness and Fulfillment (a stronger and more deeply rooted version of Happiness). This is based on the strong human tendency for Learning, Growth, Expansion, and Evolution, as well as gravitation towards the vibration of Love.

- **Attraction to our Reflection**
  The above three factors are powerful drivers. We all feel and are a part of them on some level and they represent our highest and most aspirational values, or selves. We deeply value and embrace these factors, both with our internal narratives, as well as what we project, or reflect, of ourselves to the outside world. Based on this, we are attracted to the people and/or communities that we feel best represent these qualities, as they are reflections of what we aspire *to see in ourselves*.

The above are fundamental forces that literally move and shape human behavior. They are our most aspirational values as human beings.

If company leaders and organizations embrace the depth of the above Simple Truths and then reflect it through their brand identities to augment strong and profitable business models, a greater segment of the population will be drawn to these companies, either as Customers, Employees and/or general Stakeholders.

If an organization can align its brand identity with these forces, for the right reasons, victories will surface, growth will occur, strategic advantage that is extremely hard-to-copy will emerge, and increased levels of profitability will be the result, either through enhanced sales and market share, reduced costs, or all of the above.

CHAPTER 3

The Problem
(the Opportunity, and Your
Rewards)

The Problem
(the Opportunity, and Your Rewards)

The Problem
The vast majority of company brands out there do not represent people as human beings or reflect the Simple Truths we just covered. The brand identities and subsequent messaging that most companies put out is one-dimensional and only represent the superficial aspects of human needs. While this approach definitely works, it does not align with where most people ultimately want to go anyway.

I can postulate three reasons why executives within knowledge-based companies do not dive deeper with their brand identities.

Time
Everyone knows how busy work life is for people at every level of a knowledge-based organization, especially for executives. Most of the time, we are trying to keep our heads above water with our deliverables and do not have the time to look at the big picture or to even have our gaze focus there for a brief time. It, therefore, becomes very easy for weeks, months and years to pass by without any real thought about what makes our organizational brand identity amazing, from the inside out.

Apathy
Because time can play such a central role in whether (or not) leaders or executives can focus on creating or facilitating a world-class brand identity, it can very easily be categorized as lower-priority and not worth our time, even though we know otherwise.

This sentiment can very easily become embedded individually and collectively within organizations to the point where leaders become apathetic. After all, when there are so many other things to focus on, how can brand identity be important? Because of this apathy, simple, one-dimensional and superficial fixes will take the place of where true potential could be realized.

<u>Fear</u>
The last factor is Fear. Why? Because when you start to dig deeper into what truly motivates and engages us as human beings, whether on the Customer, Employee, or Stakeholder side of things, the first realization you will have is that you are going to need to be authentic. You are going to need to be real. No more facades, no more phony narratives, no more superficiality.

When you are dealing with the superficial, it is easily manageable. When you dig deeper and begin to cultivate people's multifaceted sides, you are venturing into waters that you have not yet charted, and that unknown definitely triggers anxiety, and ultimately fear. This is why it may seem easier to keep things simple. But remember, people have their real needs, based on the Simple Truths, and these are not going anywhere.

In addition to the fear of the unknown, there is the fear of commitment. After all, once you make the choice to truly embrace a powerful brand identity, and what that really means for your organization, you will have to commit yourself totally. If you say that you are committed to the authentic, get your Customers, Employees, and Stakeholders engaged with that notion, only to re-embrace the superficial, you will absolutely destroy more value than you create. This will erode trust beyond measure and lose your organization high-value Customers and Employees, and alienate Stakeholders.

So, the above points are the three main reasons why organizations and leaders normally shy away from developing a brand identity that is truly powerful and compelling. Again, this is not just where the Customer interface is concerned, but where Employee and Stakeholder engagement are concerned as well.

Your Opportunity
Keep in mind that the brand identities of the vast majority of companies out there, big or small, are not supplying the *real needs* that their Customers, Employees, and Stakeholders are demanding. So, if there is a clear demand, as well as a clear undersupply, this represents a clear opportunity.

The question is: do you, as the facilitator or your company's brand identity and messaging, want to be associated with the superficial just to play it safe? Or do you want to take your brand to new levels of greatness where vast oceans of opportunity and additional growth await? This is where you get to decide if you really are a forward-thinking, inspired and brave leader.

Your Rewards
The entire purpose of creating, or strengthening, the foundational essence for your company's brand identity is to facilitate deep and meaningful engagement with your Customers, Employees, and Stakeholders. If you can do this, your rewards will be the following:

- Increased demand for your goods or services
- Increased profitability
- Decreased costs
- Entire oceans of new growth potential
- Powerful, hard-to-copy strategic advantages over your industry peers who don't "get" why all this is important in the first place.

If you like what you have read thus far, and want to go the distance, it is now time to set the Ground Rules for your company's success.

CHAPTER 4

Ground Rules

Ground Rules

To create a world-class brand identity, you are going to have to align with the *real needs* of your Customers, Employees, and Stakeholders. In order to do this, you are going to have to follow the following Ground Rules. If you can play to these rules, then you will derive maximum benefit from the How-to section.

Ground Rule #1: Authenticity is King

Take some time, right now, to stop and consider the depth of the word "authentic" or "authenticity" when it is applied to a person. After a few moments, consider your level of authenticity. Are you true to yourself and others? Are you trustworthy based on your level of authenticity? Do people get what they see? Are you grounded in a commitment to truth?

Now ask yourself, to whom do people more effortlessly gravitate? One who is deeply authentic, or someone who is not?

One more question for you: What kind of company would a Customer, Employee, or Stakeholder find the most appealing: one that is fiercely committed to being authentic at all levels of its organizational DNA? Or one that has no indication that they even know what this means in the first place?

Always keep in mind that most people are multifaceted, multidimensional and have the fundamental need for love, happiness, and growth (the Simple Truths). To really have a world-class brand identity, your organization has to represent these qualities, authentically, on all levels.

And by this, I don't mean only on paper. Your organization's authenticity needs to be a *feeling*. It needs to *feel* fulfilling and nourishing. Authenticity is the key to all of this. That is why it is the #1 Ground Rule.

Ground Rule #2: Open your mind to limitless potentials, and then boil them down to workable, measurable solutions.

The universe is vast. Creation itself is incredible. Life is precious, and it is short. In either creating your brand identity, or reimagining it, put yourself in this mind space. Your thinking will be more expansive, and you will open yourself up to potentials that did not exist before.

That said, we will need to re-ground ourselves at some point with workable ideas that can be tested and measured for maximum effectiveness before integrating them into a formal brand identity.

The main point is to think big, with your most aspirational mindset, but to have the end-goal of deriving workable, measurable solutions.

Ground Rule #3: Have fun and get others involved!

Having fun is essential to any creative endeavor. It brings a lifeforce energy that delivers powerful results. Of course, it is even more fun when others are having fun with you!

In creating or reimagining your brand identity, make sure to set up a scenario that integrates ground rules #1 and #2 with the element of fun and the focus on gaining collective insights. This would include getting colleagues, Customers, Employees, and even Stakeholders involved in a structured way, testing to see what works best and then ultimately creating your company's brand identity. In fact, for each of the proceeding stages of creating, or refreshing, your brand identity, making sure to include your colleagues, Customers, Employees and Stakeholders in a structured process is essential.

Now, with the Simple Truths, Your Opportunity and Rewards in mind, and Ground Rules 1, 2 and 3 set in stone, let's begin creating, or reimagining your organizational brand identity.

CHAPTER 5

★ ★ ★

Your How-To Guide
A Step-by-Step Process for Creating a World-Class Brand Identity

★ ★ ★

Your How-To Guide
A Step-by-Step Process for Creating a World-class Brand Identity

Step 1:
Categorizing Your Three Principal Market Segments

For the purposes of creating a world-class brand identity, it is essential to categorize your market into three distinct segments. This is because we want to be able to identify the *real needs* of these segments, which we will map out in just a bit. These segments are as follows:

1. Your Customer
   a. The person whose business you want to gain, or already have.
   b. The person who wants to be inspired and brand-loyal.
   c. The person who will most likely tell loads of people about your brand if you can deliver on your brand identity's promise.
2. Your Employee
   a. The person who works for your company, interfaces with your customer and/or delivers the brand identity promise.
   b. The person whose maximum productive and creative engagement you need in order to outperform your industry peers.
   c. The person you want to stay as loyal to your company as possible (if they are highly engaged).
   d. The person who will proudly tell their friends, family, and community how awesome it is to work for your company.

3. Your Stakeholder
    a. Neither a Customer nor an Employee, but rather a person who is either directly or indirectly affected by your company's operations.
    b. The person who stays silent until you give them a powerful need to speak up.
    c. The person with the ability to spread the gospel about your company, or to spread bad word-of-mouth.

Step 2:
Ascertain Your "Why", What You Stand For and/or Your Messianic Sense of Purpose

What are your company's principles as an organization? Yes, you want to make money. A lot of it. That said, keep in mind that you'll be far more effective in your pursuit of profit if your Why, What You Stand For and/or Messianic Sense of Purpose is highly compelling and deeply embedded in your organizational DNA (and by that extension your brand identity). After all, people want to be inspired and they love a good story. Your "Why", What You Stand For and/or Your Messianic Sense of Purpose will come into play in a powerful way when we get to the Qunity Vortex™ tool a little later on.

Exercise #1
With the Simple Truths and Ground Rules in mind, create, or modify, your company's Why, What You Stand For and/or your Messianic Sense of Purpose.

Step 3:
Map Out the *Real Needs* of Your Customers, Employees, and Stakeholders

With any kind of promotion, it is important to research the stated needs of your Customer. That much is obvious. But what about the *real* needs of your **Customers**? And since your **Employees** are the ones who ultimately reflect your company's brand on every level through action and delivery, what are their real needs? And what are the real needs of the **Stakeholders**? Do all these needs correlate well with and reflect each other? And how does your company's brand identity tie all these real needs together to provide a brand promise that is compelling, vibrant, dynamic, multidimensional and even nourishing?

It is absolutely essential to understand what drives your Customers, Employees, and Stakeholders - on multiple levels. By this I mean it is important to understand what their *real* needs are and how they relate to the brand identity of your organization.

To map out your Customer, Employee and Stakeholder needs, we are going to use a modified version of Maslow's Hierarchy of Needs. These needs will be categorized on Practical, Emotional and Aspirational levels and must be built one on top of the other. Here is a brief explanation of how each of these categories is defined, and how to structure them:

Practical Needs (the foundation)
Practical Needs are the foundation upon which the other needs will be built. This is because the Practical Needs are the absolute first thing that must be delivered before the other two needs can be met effectively.

Practical Needs are all about safety, process, consistency, quality, structure, efficiency, overall fair exchange etc.

Emotional Needs
When you have a strong foundational basis in meeting the Practical Needs of your Customers, Employees, and Stakeholders, you can focus on meeting their Emotional Needs.

Emotional Needs are all about how your company makes people *feel*. After all, humans are deeply emotional beings and these needs are serious business. They also tie directly into the Simple Truths outlined above.

Again, you cannot deliver on the Emotional Needs of your Customers, Employees, and Stakeholders if the Practical Needs are not met first.

Aspirational Needs
Aspirational Needs are all about leaving a lasting legacy, serving the greater good, wanting your life to have meaning, contributing to the overall health of the whole environment, etc. This can be referred to as many things, like CSR (Corporate Social Responsibility), corporate philanthropy, corporate citizenship, sustainable development, corporate accountability, creating shared value (CSV) etc.

I choose to use the word "Aspirational" because it means something much more than the standard industry jargon to which we have become overly accustomed, and risk tuning out. For the purposes of creating a world-class brand identity, one that really stands out from a crowded field of unending sameness, using deep and powerful words is essential. It also draws in your focus, because this is where your deeper principles, values, and philosophies get to come out and play.

Where your brand identity is involved, the Aspirational Need is important because we are all finite beings and most of us want to know that our lives matter, and that we will have left a positive imprint on this earth when we pass on. Since this is something we want for ourselves, and deeply admire when we see it in others, including in organizations, it is an important need to meet.

And in case you need some eye-opening statistics[1], check out the following:

- 78% of people want companies to address important social justice issues.
- 71% of Millennials want businesses to lead social and environmental change in the absence of government regulation, compared to 63% of all Americans.
- 87% of Americans say they would purchase a product because a company supported an issue they care about.
- 76% would refuse to buy from a company if they learn it supports an issue contrary to their own beliefs.

The moral of these statistics? Get on board with serving the greater good, through your business activities. It is what people are demanding, so supply that demand, authentically, and be a world-class brand.

Oh, and the above statistics are merely the tip of an iceberg of a legion of additional corresponding statistics that clearly indicate what the typical knowledge-based Employee is looking for in a knowledge-based organization.

At the very least...
To be moderately successful in creating or building out your brand identity, it is essential, at the very least, to meet the Practical and Emotional needs of your Customers, Employees, and Stakeholders.

Be cautious
Providing the Aspirational Need is optional (but highly recommendable). Why? Because the Aspirational Need is an area where you are adding an enhanced element of risk. This

---

* http://www.conecomm.com/research-blog/2017-csr-study

is simply because people tend to be weary of for-profit companies talking about how they serve the greater good when a profit motive is involved. There is an underlying cynicism here and this is where the risk lies.

You should only look into providing the Aspirational Need for your Customers, Employees, and Stakeholders if you are willing to commit to it totally. It has to be something that your organization can continue to stay passionate about over the long haul. If you are serious about it and place focus on quality delivery, you will present the brand identity trifecta of excellence that your Customers, Employees, and Stakeholders not only want, but need, from your company's brand identity. If you put together something half-baked or pay lip service only where the Aspirational element is concerned, you will destroy more value than you create.

With all of the above in mind, let's take a look at what some of the Practical, Emotional and Aspirational needs could be for the Customer, Employee, and Stakeholder categories.

Practical Needs

Practical **Customer** Needs
It is important to map out exactly what the Customer's needs are on the Practical level if they choose to frequent your establishment or do business with your organization at all. Relevant questions might be the following:

- Are your prices reasonable given the stated quality of the product?
- Is your place a relatively clean and safe environment?
- Are your Employees relatively approachable, friendly and knowledgeable about your product?
- Are your payment options what the Customer wants or needs?
- Can people find and connect with your company easily?

- Does the general exchange of the good for the service meet basic practical requirements for your Customer to feel as though the Practical need has been met?

This list could go on, but you know your business best so make sure to spend time mapping out all the aspects your Customer needs in order to feel as though the Practical exchange of their money for your goods or services has been met and is satisfactory.

Practical **Employee** Needs

With regard to the Practical needs of your Employees, it is important to map out what their Practical Needs are in working for your company or organization. For example, the main operative words that should be in play are "structure", "stability", "safety", "fairness", "learning new skills", "opportunities for professional advancement", etc. Here are some of the questions that need affirmative 'yes' answers:

- Is there a clear structure, with clear objectives, at all levels of your organization?
- Are all people held accountable for their deliverables?
- Are people paid fairly and, hopefully, with proper, livable benefits?
- Basically, do your Employees feel *stable*, and *safe*, in your work environment?
- Is the system fair?
- Are there opportunities for professional growth and advancement?

Again, the above are just a few of the questions that need strong 'yes' answers in order for your Employees to feel that their Practical needs are met within your company.

Practical **Stakeholder** Needs

The Stakeholder's Practical need is simple: Be legal, safe, ethical, fair and environmentally honorable/sustainable. Most companies are exactly this, or at least they intend to be. To state the obvious, if a company does not represent these elements, no amount of effort to meet the Emotional Need will be successful. In fact, to do so would do more harm than good, in that the Stakeholder. and even your Customer and Employee, would become irretrievably cynical about your organization. If this happens, active disengagement, and even sabotage, are not far behind.

Exercise #2
With the Simple Truths and Ground Rules in mind, and in short sentences, write down the perceived <u>Practical</u> Needs of your company's Customer, Employee, and Stakeholder.

Emotional Needs

After you have your Customer, Employee and Stakeholder needs mapped out, it is time to move to the next level, which are the Emotional Needs. Whereas the Practical Needs create the base elements that your company needs to be successful, the Emotional Needs are where you create and associate *feelings* and *emotions* with your company's brand.

As you proceed in mapping the Emotional and Aspirational Needs of your Customers, Employees, and Stakeholders, it is critical that you remember, and internalize, the Simple Truths and Ground Rules that we laid out at the beginning of this book.

<u>Emotional **Customer** Needs</u>
How do you want your customers to *feel* about your company? In other words, think about what kinds of powerful and positive emotions there are, and then go deeper. Again, remember the Simple Truths and Ground Rules that we outlined earlier. Again, people will always be more attracted to something that reflects what they want to see *in* themselves, or want *for* themselves.

To ascertain your Customer, Employee and Stakeholder Emotional Needs, consider these following questions to trigger your own thinking on the matter:

- What kind of emotions do I want to be associated with my company?
- How will my company's Why, What-We-Stand-For or Messianic Sense of Purpose trigger those emotions in our Customers?
- How can I use the Simple Truths to create associative emotions with my company's brand?

Emotional **Employee** Needs

Employees have emotional needs too, of course. But they are a little bit different from the needs of the Customer. Being a happy worker can mean many things to many people. Many companies have "happy" employees on the surface level. For our intents and purposes, we want to take it to the next level.

Now, you may rightly say that this is an issue of overall strategy that leadership needs to initiate and support, with human resources arranging and facilitating the specifics. While this may be true, if you want to create a world-class brand identity, your people need to be fully engaged, using most or all of their creative and/or output potential.

This is where the Simple Truths directly pertain. Live them, learn them, love them. If you can deeply internalize and feel these Simple Truths to your organizational DNA's core, where your Employees' emotional growth is concerned, you are definitely on the right track towards creating your own world-class brand identity.

The question I want you to deeply consider is how you facilitate and nourish your Employees' Emotional Needs based on the Simple Truths? How do you create a work environment that provides for at least a few of these Needs? And what would be your plan for growing, strengthening and sustaining them to the point that they become deeply embedded into your company's organizational DNA on a more permanent basis?

Of course, there will be the Employee who does not care about additional fulfillment or growth. Maybe they deeply care about the Practical part of the equation and that is all they need to be deeply engaged. That is great, but we want to meet Emotional Needs as well.

Now, ask and give brief answers to questions pertaining to how your company call fulfill the Emotional Needs of your Employee. Questions might include:

- How does my company create a sense of community and belonging within the organization?
- How does my company facilitate the *personal* growth of my Employees?
- Does my company allow for my Employees to imagine, ideate, create and innovate, both as individuals and/or in groups?
- What are the aspirations of my company's Employees and how can we use my company's resources to help Employees achieve those aspirations if they really want to?

Emotional **Stakeholder** Needs

Simply said, Stakeholders want to know that your company is not only providing the Practical Needs of your Employees, but also for their Emotional Needs.

Most Stakeholders are not going to conduct their own extensive research into whether or not your company provides for these needs. But, with all the free and easily accessible information out there, like social media and the rating/reviews platforms of Yelp, Google, Facebook, Glassdoor and the like, and with more people doing their research about companies before giving the company their business, it becomes vital to ensure that you provide for the

Practical and Emotional Needs of your Stakeholder.

In addition, we have all witnessed what happens when bad corporate citizenship at the Emotional level becomes public, gains traction and blows up on media platforms - significant value can be destroyed for the offending company, sometimes irrecoverably.

But, if you can create an organizational environment the makes the authentically driven effort to fulfill the Emotional Needs of your Employees so that it becomes deeply embedded in your organizational DNA, and by extension your Brand Identity, your company will not only gain continuous credibility but facilitate fantastic word-of-mouth with your Stakeholders (which is the most effective form or marketing known to man).

Exercise #3
With the Simple Truths and Ground Rules in mind, and in short sentences, write down the perceived Emotional needs of your company's Customer, Employee, and Stakeholder.

Aspirational Needs

If you are indeed going to go for the gold and talk about how your organization is committed, wholeheartedly and authentically, towards serving the greater good through your business activities, philosophy, etc. then there is no need to categorize what this means for your Customers, Employees, Stakeholders, as it means the same thing

---

Exercise #4
With the Simple Truths and Ground Rules in mind, and in short sentences, write down the perceived Aspirational needs of your company's Customer, Employee, and Stakeholder.

Step 4
Creating a list of descriptive adjectives, nouns, key words

So far in this How-to Guide, you have categorized three market segments and identified your Why, What-We-Stand-For and/or your Messianic Sense of Purpose. You have written short sentences of the outlining Practical, Emotional and Aspirational needs of your Customers, Employees, and Stakeholders.

Step #4 in building the essence of a world-class brand identity is to take the above information and come up with a list of descriptive adjectives, nouns and/or brief key words that best encapsulate what you have come up with in exercises 2-4. These words will be used consistently for your internal and external communications to re-enforce your brand identity. The table on the following page is an example of how to structure your words.

Practical	Emotional	Aspirational
Customers	**Customers**	**Customers**
• Clean	• Inspiring	• Gives back
• Safe	• Happy	• Leaves lasting
• High-quality	• Welcoming	legacy
• Good value	• Relaxing	• Eco-friendly
• Consistent	• Stress-free	
		Employees
Employees	**Employees**	• Gives back
• Clean	• Inspiring	• Leaves lasting
• Safe	• Fun	legacy
• Well-	• Fulfilling	• Eco-friendly
structured	• Sense of	
• Clear	belonging	**Stakeholders**
expectations	• Opportunities for	• Gives back
• Fairly paid	personal growth	• Leaves lasting
• Opportunities		legacy
for	**Stakeholders**	• Eco-friendly
professional	• Inspiring	
growth	• Compelling	
Stakeholders		
• Provides		
good jobs		
• Clean		
company		
• Good		
benefits		

Step 5
Deploying The Qunity Vortex™ Tool

Based on what you have come up with in Exercises 1-4, you have a clear and concise idea of the following:

- Your Company's Why, What-We-Stand-For and/or Messianic Sense of Purpose.
- The Practical, Emotional and Aspirational Needs of your company's Customer, Employee, and Stakeholder, written in short sentences
- The descriptive adjectives, nouns and keywords that describe the Practical, Emotional and Aspirational Needs of your company's Customer, Employee, and Stakeholder.

Step 5 is deploying the Qunity Vortex™ tool.

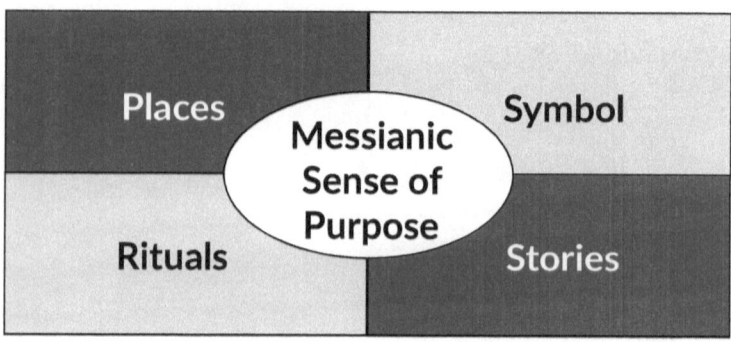

The "Qunity Vortex™" is designed to help create deep, meaningful and lasting positive associations with your brand in the minds of its target demographics. In fact, any company, organization or tightly knit society that has a powerful Why, What-We-Stand-For and/or Messianic Sense of Purpose at its core, will comprise, whether knowingly or not, Places, Symbols Rituals and Stories that surround the core 'Why' of that company or organization.

Even **without** the information you have mapped out in Exercises 1-4 above, the Qunity Vortex™ will help create powerful associations with your company in the minds of whatever demographic you want to target. So, with our final exercise, Exercise #5, you are going to refer to the information gained thus far in Exercises 1-4, and then think about what your company's cultural and/or historical assets are with regard to its Places Symbols, Rituals, and Stories.

Let's use the company Nike as an example for the effective use of the Qunity Vortex™.

Messianic Sense of Purpose
At its beginnings, Nike's goal was to come from nothing and overtake Adidas as the world's largest and most influential shoe company, which seemed like an impossible task at the time (Messianic Sense of Purpose).

Places
Nike was born at Hayward Field in Eugene, Oregon where there was already a well-established and well-renown history of track and field (Place).

Symbols
- Nike's "Swoosh".
- One day, the Head Coach of the University of Oregon at the time, Bill Bowerman, poured melted rubber into his wife's waffle iron and the first waffle sole for a running shoe was born (Symbol).

Rituals
Every day, Steve Prefontaine, one of the fastest and most charismatic distance runners ever, and one of the first people to wear the waffle shoe, would take a run along the Willamette River in his Nike shoes that Bill Bowerman had made by hand using the waffle sole (Rituals).

<u>Stories</u>
All of the above provide narrative-rich information by which Nike has built one of the most impactful and compelling brands in the world.

While Nike's Messianic Sense of Purpose might have needed to change after its goal of overtaking Adidas was achieved, its initial Places, Symbols, Rituals and Stories have been consistently repeated and expanded upon throughout the company's 40+ year history. And there have been additional Places, Symbols, Rituals, and Stories that have been integrated into Nike's narrative to add strength and dynamism to its overall brand and brand identity.

Exercise #5
With the above as an example, take some time to write down your company's relevant Places, Symbols, and Rituals. Do your best to correlate these items with the information you have come up with thus far in exercises 1-4. Once you have done this, you are ready to begin creating some highly impactful Stories that are in line with your burgeoning world-class brand identity.

Step 6
Creating Your Brand Identity Statement

Let's review what you have created thus far:

1. Your company's Why, What-We-Stand-For and/or Messianic Sense of Purpose
2. Described, in short sentences, the Practical, Emotional and Aspirational Needs of your Customer, Employee and Stakeholder.
3. Your company's descriptive adjectives/keywords that touch upon the Practical, Emotional and Aspirational levels.
4. Your Qunity Vortex™

Now you can create a structured and highly focused Brand Identity Statement with a summation of the above four components. Your Brand Identity Statement should be no more than 2-3 pages.

Due Diligence
Before codifying your Brand Identity Statement, it is highly recommendable that you test that it resonates well with your Customers, Employees, and Stakeholders. If you do indeed want to do your due diligence, which again, is highly recommended, you should first conduct interviews and/or focus groups. Your Customers, Employees, and Stakeholders will have loads of insightful information that will allow you to further refine your Brand Identity Statement for maximum effectiveness.

With the information and insights gained from your interviews and/or focus groups, you should then administer online surveys to reflect, reinforce or call into question the insights gained from your interviews or focus groups.

In creating the questions for both your focus groups and surveys, make sure that you structure your questions to correspond to the Practical, Emotional and Aspirational needs of Customers, Employee, and Stakeholders. Once you have done your due diligence, you can formalize your Brand Identity Statement.

Once this is done, the next tasks are to reinforce it with your Customers, Employees, and Stakeholders through your company's marketing and communications activities, and the actual delivery of your products or services.

The Brand Identity Diagnostic
Depending upon the size of your organization, as well as where your branding activities are at the time where your Customers, Employees, and Stakeholders are concerned, you will want to conduct a Brand Identity Diagnostic once every 3-12 months.

This is simply to measure the effectiveness of the delivery of your Brand Identity's promise.

Again, this is done through interviews, focus groups and surveys, where the questions are categorized at the Practical, Emotional, and Aspirational levels. With these insights, you can adjust your Brand Identity Statement, and then adjust the internal and external communications as needed.

CHAPTER 6

Concluding Remarks

Concluding Remarks

To conclude this book, it is important to review why it was written in the first place. This is best summed up by remembering the Problem, reviewing the Solution, and then illustrating the Benefits you will experience.

Problem

The brands and brand identities of far too many companies around the world are not meeting the *real* needs of the Customer, Employee and Stakeholder. This represents a significant demand that is being undersupplied. This also represents an opportunity for truly brave, inspired and forward-thinking leaders and companies.

Your Opportunity

The solution is to supply the demand. This means digging deep into the human condition to figure out how to meet the real needs of our Customers, Employees, and Stakeholders. For this, we need to:

- Keep in mind the Simple Truths
- Follow the Ground Rules
- Clearly define your compelling Why/What You Stand For/Messianic Sense of Purpose
- Map out the real Practical, Emotional, and Aspirational Needs of your Customers, Employees, and Stakeholders.
- Identify the Places, Symbols, Rituals, and Stories that will reinforce the associations you want your Customers, Employees and Stakeholders to have about your company.
- Boil it all down to a powerful, brilliantly simple, 2-3 page Brand Identity Statement from which you can weave and

communicate powerful narratives that create true engagement.

Your Rewards

Because your company brand identity will be supplying the *real* needs of your Customers, Employees and Stakeholders, you will enjoy incredibly hard-to-copy strategic advantages over your industry peers. The benefits of this will include the following:

- Increased demand for your goods or services
- Decreased costs and increased profitability
- Dramatically increased brand-loyalty from your Customers
- Dramatically increased ability to attract, and keep, highly engaged Employees
- Entire oceans of new growth potential
- Powerful, hard-to-copy strategic advantages over your industry peers who don't "get" why all this is important in the first place.

Yet perhaps the greatest benefit is how *you will feel* in working with a company that is the embodiment of the Simple Truths discussed at the beginning of this book. Again, these are the elemental components that drive the human condition. If you can align with and channel these forces, using the structure outlined in this book, you will create workable and powerful narratives that will form the basis of not only an extremely hard-to-copy, world-class brand identity, but a world-class organization as a whole.

Good luck. Have fun. Enjoy!

www.ingramcontent.com/pod-product-compliance
Lightning Source LLC
Chambersburg PA
CBHW030544220526
45463CB00007B/2975